CONTENTS

ME AND MY MONSTER

RICK DOBBERTIN'S

SURFACE ORBITER

Radio antennas

Weight: 9 tons

Have you driven your milk tanker today?

16.5-inch aluminum wheel with 35-inch-diameter all-terrain tire

GPS antenna

Radar
antenna

Air intake

Spare tires (three more
on the other side)

Four-wheel drive through
front and rear axles (third
axle only supports weight)

Overall length: 32½ feet

Custom-built
stainless-steel
chassis

Rick Dobbertin wanted a vehicle he could drive on land or water, so he
built one from a stainless-steel tank trailer that was used to haul milk.
Powered by a 6.5-liter turbocharged GM diesel engine, the nine-ton
Surface Orbiter can hit 70 miles per hour on land and scoots along at 8 knots
(about 9.2 miles per hour) on water. Controls and communication and navigation
electronics are in the front compartment; the engine room and sleeping quarters
are in the middle; and the kitchen—complete with sink and microwave—and
restroom are in the back. It is registered for land as a "Custom House on
Wheels" and for water as the motor yacht *Perseverance*. In three years Rick
drove it through 38 states, 28 countries, and the Panama Canal. ◎

ME AND MY MONSTER

JERRY BOWERS'S
HOT ROD SCHOOL BUS

Airfoil
(not required on
ordinary school buses)

WANNA BE COOL... STAY IN SCHOOL!

Jerry wanted to keep the original-style
doors: he had to make nine cuts in
them to fit them into the new opening

Never be late for school again!

If you're late getting to the stop for this bus, you probably won't be able to run fast enough to catch it—and the driver will never hear you shouting "stop!" over the roar of the supercharged engine. Jerry Bowers spent five years building this wicked 1949 Ford school bus. It's $3^1/_2$ feet lower and 7 feet shorter than the original bus, and it now sits on a front-wheel drive Cadillac Eldorado chassis. Jerry travels across the country in his hot rod bus to deliver a message to all kids: If you want to be cool, stay in school. "We need one of those," said one teacher at a stop in San Jose, California. "That is the coolest school bus in the world, hands down." ◎

Four-barrel carburetors

Supercharger

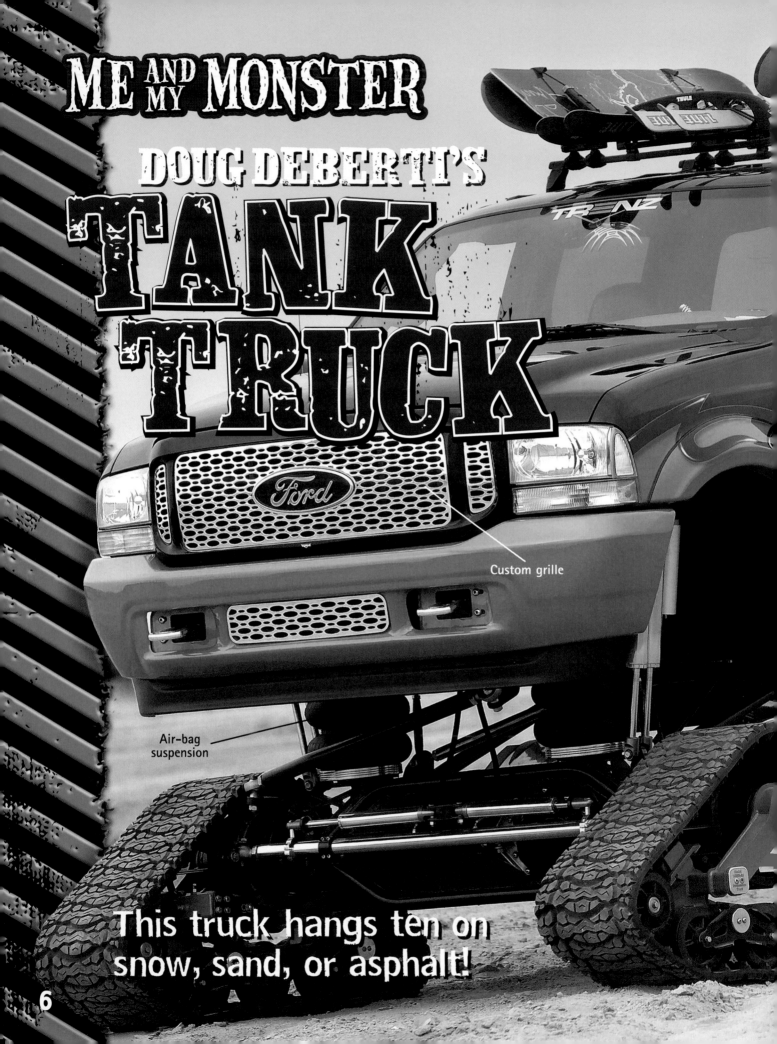

ME AND MY MONSTER

DOUG DEBERTI'S
TANK TRUCK

Custom grille

Air-bag suspension

This truck hangs ten on snow, sand, or asphalt!

> *"What I really like doing is the one-off stuff. I'm most creative in coming up with something really different. We have our own style. I refuse to copy anything. I like our stuff to stand out."*
> — DOUG DEBERTI

Runs on track units or wheels and tires

Custom suspension arms cut from two-inch-thick polished stainless steel oug Deberti's Tank Truck pickup can go just about anywhere. When Doug has gone as far as he can on the huge off-road tires (shown *below*), he can install crawler tracks in place of the wheels and tires (shown in the opening photo). The truck is legal to drive on the street with the track units because they have rubber treads. It can go about 50 miles per hour on the tracks. Custom-built air suspension allows Doug to raise or lower the truck, even while it is moving. Doug's personal garage (shown *above*) is like a big toy chest full of great cars, trucks, and offroad vehicles. The black Lamborghini at the front right is his favorite, but he drives a customized purple Hummer most of the time.

The work area in his home garage (shown *right*) has enough tools and equipment to keep any gearhead happy.

Wheels mounted, track units stowed in pickup bed

Four-wheel (or four-track) drive

Doug started making parts and customizing trucks after he graduated from high school. For a few years he worked at other jobs to pay his bills while he built up the business. Now he has a 35,000-square-foot factory and employs more than a hundred people. "I've designed over 3,000 parts that we mass distribute everywhere," Doug says. "We're now machining parts around the clock seven days a week." Do adults come up with all the creative ideas? Doug says not. "My 12-year-old son, Shane, already designed a rearview mirror that is in production right now—it's pretty cool." ◉

DEAN JEFFRIES'S
LANDMASTER

Rocket launchers

Remote-control cannons

Farm-equipment tire, 38 inches in diameter

All-terrain triangular wheel carriage

Overall length: 35 feet

The Landmaster is one of many vehicles Dean Jeffries built for the movies. He built Landmaster for a 1977 film. He borrowed the design for the triangular wheel carriages from an idea for a military all-terrain vehicle. When the Landmaster is on the move, all 12 wheels turn, but only eight are on the ground at a time. If one of the wheels on the ground hits a rock or other large object, its triangular carriage rotates and the wheel on top comes down onto the obstacle and crawls over it. "Not much will stop it," Dean says of the 11-ton machine. ◉

Shock and awe—
Hollywood style

Escape hatches

Cannon

> *"We built it to run through walls, tear up buildings, go through just about anything. The steel in the nose is 3/8 inch thick."*
> — DEAN JEFFRIES

Boarding door

ME AND MY MONSTER

HYLER BRACEY'S

BIG HORN

KAHLENBERG

Really big horn

All the bells and whistles—and then some

Custom-built chassis and body,
27 feet long

Weight: 9½ tons

Bells

Whistles

Various pressure
gauges

Hyler Bracey and his wife, Cass Flagg, call their unusual vehicle Big Horn. That could be because it has 4 ship's horns (including the largest one in the world), a foghorn, and 18 other horns from trains, boats, trucks, and even a submarine. And that's not all: It has 55 antique steam whistles, 51 air whistles, 2 steam sirens from U.S. Navy destroyers, and 21 bells that came off of everything from a fire truck to a trolley. If the sound isn't enough to get your attention, it also has lights—175 feet of neon lights, 76 feet of rope lights, and 20 powerful strobes—and 2 smoke machines. ◉

Boyd Coddington

Fiberglass body and fenders

When it comes to cool jobs, Boyd Coddington's tops the list. He builds hot rods and custom cars, like ZZ Top's Cadzzilla, for a living. His Boydster III design (shown) is based on the style of the 1933–34 Ford roadster. Boyd also sells custom parts so people can build hot rods themselves. Boyd started working on cars at home in Idaho when he was 13. By the time he graduated from high school he had owned and tinkered with half a dozen cars. After an apprenticeship, he became a machinist and moved to California. He opened his hot rod business in 1978. Boyd is considered the originator of the billet wheel, a wheel machined from a solid chunk of aluminum. Between building hot rods and custom cars— more than 300 of them—and manufacturing wheels, Boyd has become one of the biggest names in hot rodding. ⊙

351-cubic-inch Ford V-8 under hood

Custom grille with the look of a 1934 Ford

Brake caliper

Hot rods are Boyd's business

Billet wheel

Brake disc

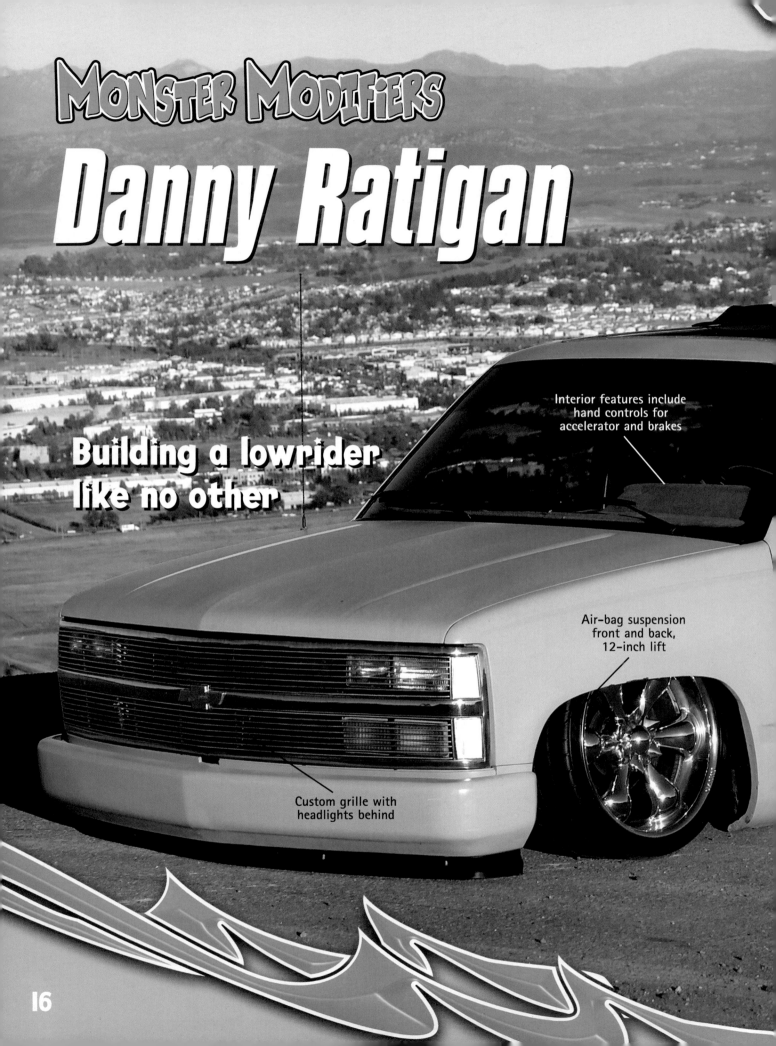

MONSTER MODIFIERS
Danny Ratigan

Building a lowrider like no other

Interior features include hand controls for accelerator and brakes

Air-bag suspension front and back, 12-inch lift

Custom grille with headlights behind

"I can weld, I can do bodywork, I can cut and grind—anything I can reach I can do myself."

— *Danny Ratigan*

Sliding fabric sunroof

Door handles removed (solenoids operate the latches through remote control or pushbuttons)

Danny Ratigan's '93 Chevy Silverado has the usual lowrider stuff—airbag suspension, custom wheels, a smoothed body—and one not-so-usual modification—hand controls. Danny, who works in construction, is a paraplegic. "I was riding in a car when I was 13 years old," he says. "We got hit by another car and I lost the use of my legs." But that hasn't kept him from working on cars. Danny does a lot of the work himself, and his friends at Temecula Rod and Custom help with the rest. ◉

MONSTER MODIFIERS
Calvin Wan

Drifting along like a roaring, tire-smoking, side-sliding tumbleweed

Custom fascia

Full roll cage
inside

Airfoil

Rear–wheel
drive

FALKEN

E2EK1EL

MOTOREX
NISSAN
WEST
APEX
DS GIKE
WOLF TECH
RAYS
ENGINEER
Auto

APEXi. E2EKIE

MOTOR

Performance
wheel with
10 spokes

Custom
side skirt

Performance wheel
with five spokes

" *I've been fascinated with cars*
for as long as I can remember. **"**
— *Calvin Wan*

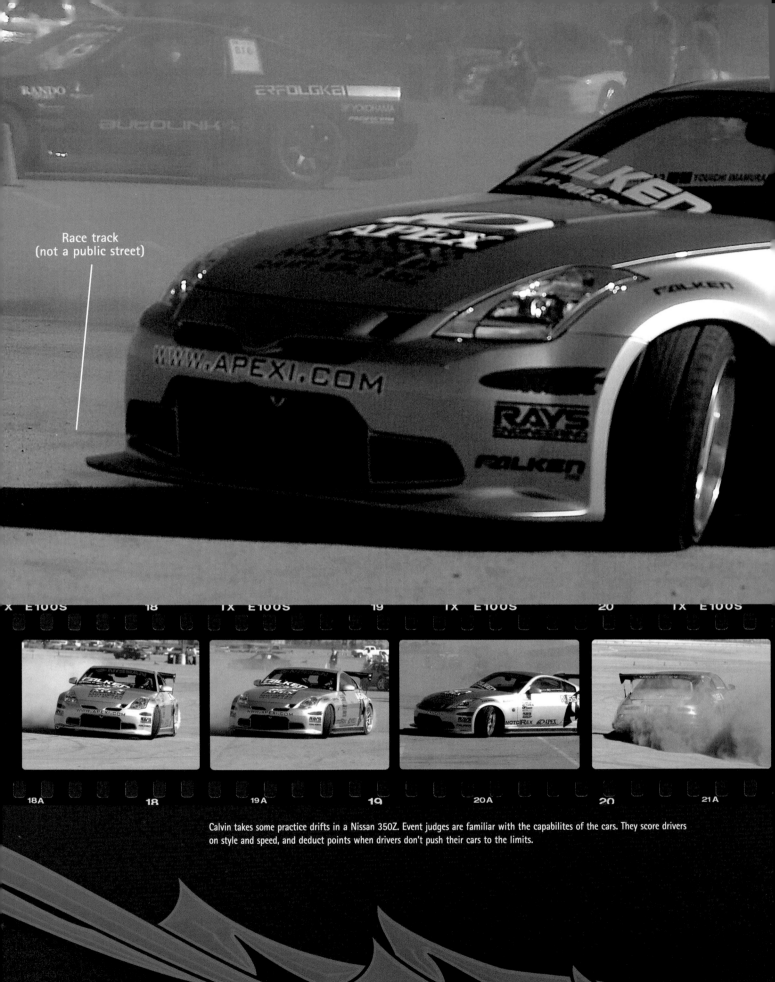

Race track
(not a public street)

Calvin takes some practice drifts in a Nissan 350Z. Event judges are familiar with the capabilites of the cars. They score drivers on style and speed, and deduct points when drivers don't push their cars to the limits.

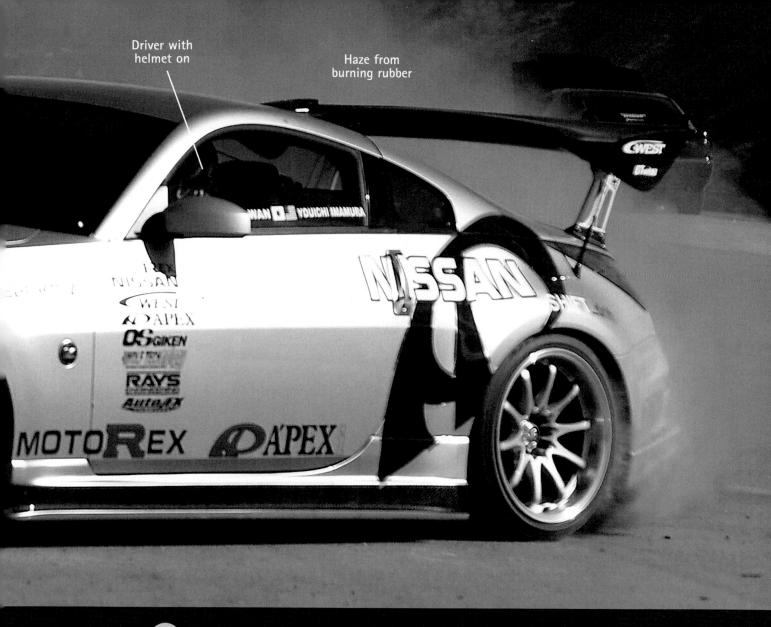

Driver with helmet on

Haze from burning rubber

Calvin Wan, a 26-year-old San Franciscan, found out about drifting through Japanese magazines and videos. Drifting started about 15 years ago when Japanese street racers discovered that driving their cars in controlled drifts—or slides—at relatively low speed produced a lot of noise, tire smoke, and excitement. Later, with support from manufacturers and the media, it grew into a sport so popular that top Japanese drivers were treated like rock stars. In the United States, the first grand prix of drifting drew 10,000 fans at Southern California's Irwindale Speedway in 2003.

Cars for drifting must have rear-wheel drive, but the way the vehicle is set up and the driver's skill are more important than power or speed. In fact, too much speed can quickly turn a drift into a spin. "It's a sport where the little guy has a chance against the big guys," says one drifting enthusiast.

Calvin, who owns a company specializing in car graphics, teaches the sport through some drifting clubs in California. It's just another part of his longtime love of cars. "Even before I could read I was already looking at pictures of cars in magazines and brochures. Over the years I've had many auto-related jobs, such as installing tires and working as a valet-parking trainer for a hotel in San Francisco," the tire-scorcher says. ⊚

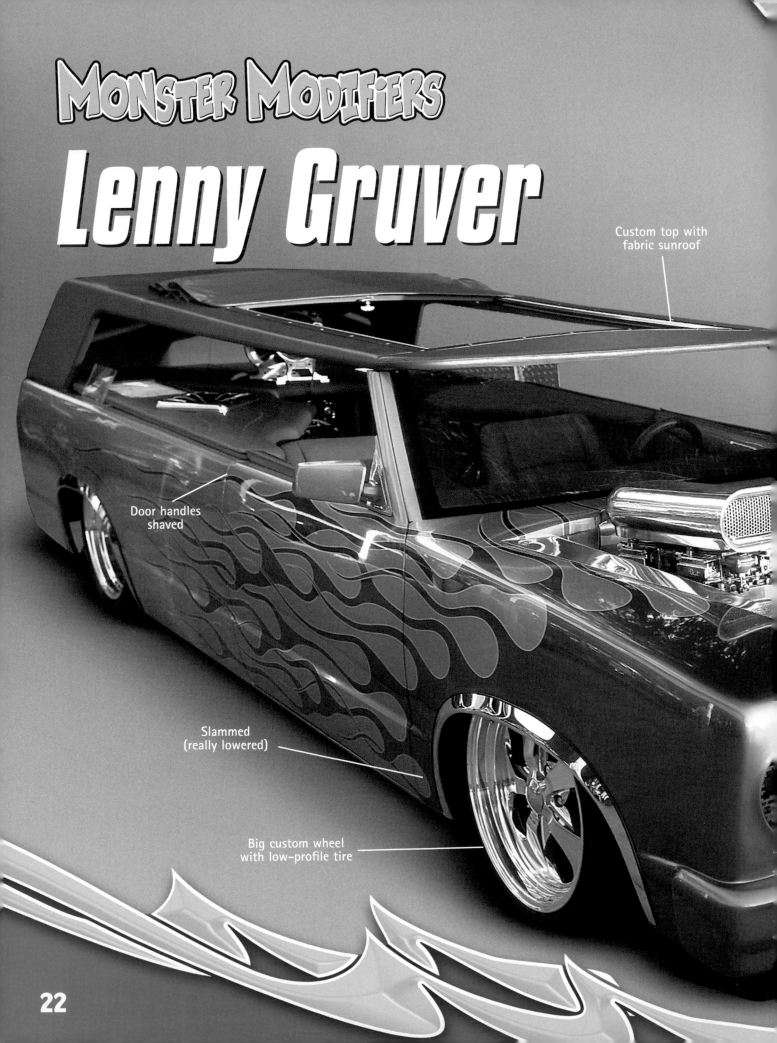

MONSTER MODIFIERS
Lenny Gruver

Custom top with fabric sunroof

Door handles shaved

Slammed (really lowered)

Big custom wheel with low-profile tire

When Lenny Gruver gets off work at his regular job, he goes to another job—running his own customizing shop. His own Chevy S-10 Extended Cab pickup shows what he can do. "I bought it brand new to cut it up," Lenny recalls. "I drove it two miles from the dealer and the very next weekend I lowered it. Then about every six months for the next five years I did something different to it. I did all the normal lowrider stuff. I've just worked on it year after year," he says. The 2.5-liter Pontiac engine puts out 310 horsepower, he says, and the interior is leather and ostrich skin with German square-weave carpet. Like most hot rodders, Lenny got the bug at an early age, in his case from his father. "He took me to car shows before I even knew what was going on." Lenny says. " Lenny and his dad built Lenny's first car together. ◉

Fully detailed engine compartment with custom-built panels, no hood

" *I do everything and anything you want: hydraulics, air, bodydrops—stuff like that.* **"**
— *Lenny Gruver*

Custom grille opening with 1957 Chevy grille bar

Tank like pressure fuel tank on early dragsters

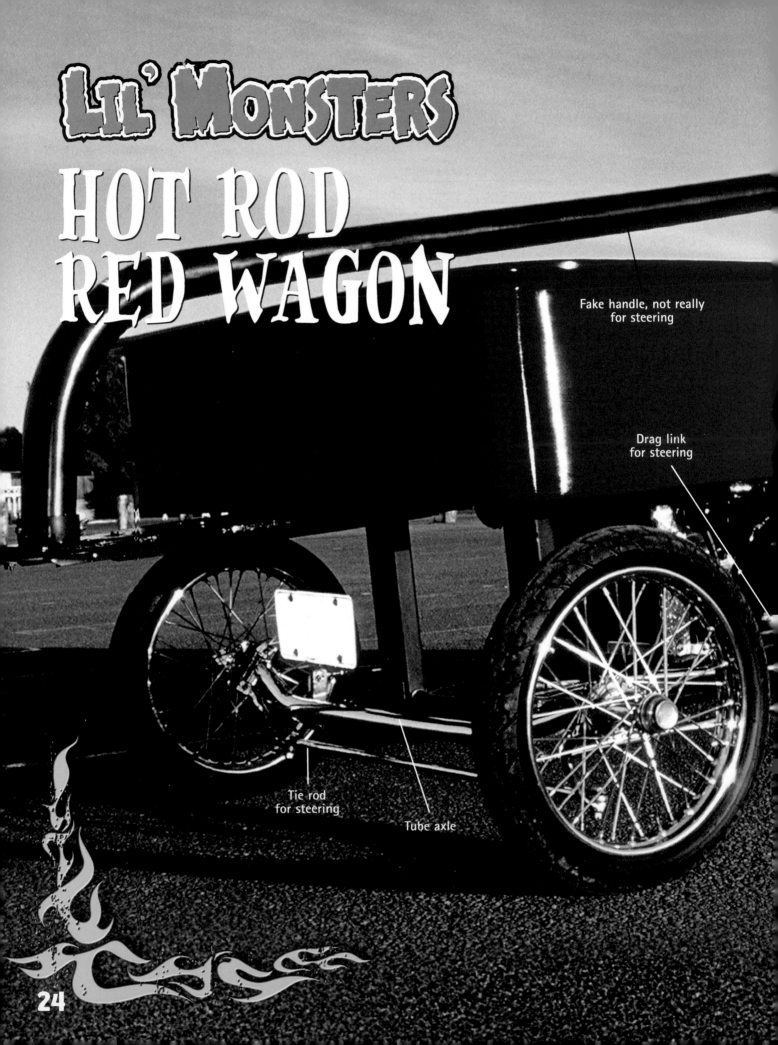

LiL' Monsters
HOT ROD RED WAGON

Fake handle, not really for steering

Drag link for steering

Tie rod for steering

Tube axle

RADIO FLYER

Steel-tube chassis

Pitman arm for steering

Big meats (fat tires) on back

Bob Castaneda and his cousin, Art Baker, originally wanted to build a standard T-bucket roadster. They made a frame of steel tubing, put a Chevy engine in it, and put fat tires on the back and skinny ones on the front. But then Bob got the wagon idea. "I wanted to build something really different, and the more I thought about it, the more I liked it—so I went with it," Bob says. After a year of working on weekends, it was done. When the removable windshield is installed, the wagon is legal to drive on the street. Now Bob plans to make the whole body removable so he can put on other bodies. "I've got a couple of other ideas for bodies that I'm going to build," he says. "They're all interchangeable. I have this car because I like to have fun. I'm adventurous, and, like other artists, I do it partly for the attention," he says. ◉

LIL' MONSTERS

Throttle plate

Supercharger drive pulley

Idler pulley

Drive belt

Fuel injection lines

Supercharger

Intake manifold

Chrysler hemi engine

Jim Asbury, ready for a quick round of golf

Crankshaft pulley

Studebaker bullet nose

HEMI GOLF CART

"**O**utrageous is OK" is one of the principles of building monster machines. Take Jim Asbury's golf cart, for example. In the first place, most golf carts don't look like a 1950–51 Studebaker, complete with the Studie's famous bullet-nose styling. Second, golf carts have small engines, like you might find on a riding lawnmower or garden tractor. Jim's has a blown Chrysler hemi instead. Jim should be able to haul his clubs from the tee to the green on a 440-yard hole (1,320 feet or 1/4 mile, the length of a dragstrip) in five seconds or so, if he can get any traction on the grass. In truth, Jim's hemi golf cart is just a mock-up. But the real thing is under construction. Someday golfers on some course may hear "Fore!" followed by a roar. ◉

MONSTER TOUCH
BODY BUILDING

From simple trim removal to complete restyling, custom bodywork creates the most radical change in a car's looks. It can also cost the most.

Bolt-on accessories like grilles, headlight covers, or taillight lenses can give a car a different look. Wings, spoilers, ground-effect kits, valences and fascias, scoops, and other styling features are also available ready-made. The term "bolt-on," however, doesn't always cover the full extent of labor necessary to get the pieces onto a car and looking right. The work sometimes calls for bonding and molding the parts to the body and repainting the area.

Radical customizing calls for classic bodywork techniques using metal or fiberglass. (Some are shown on the 1949 Mercury *below*.) Many jobs call for professional-level skills and a well-equipped shop. Nonetheless, amateurs create some of the slickest custom bodywork seen on the streets and in shows.

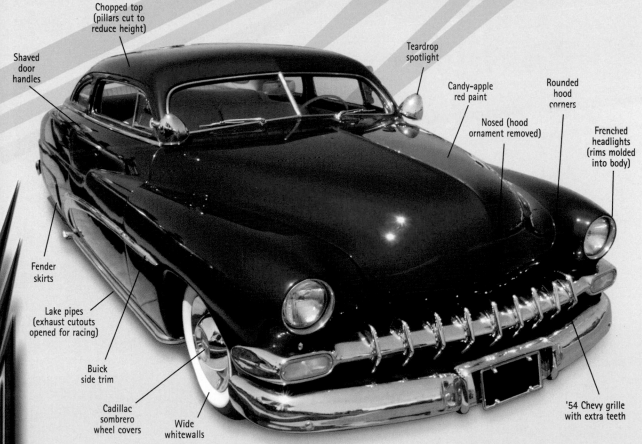

Chopped top (pillars cut to reduce height)

Shaved door handles

Teardrop spotlight

Candy-apple red paint

Rounded hood corners

Nosed (hood ornament removed)

Frenched headlights (rims molded into body)

Fender skirts

Lake pipes (exhaust cutouts opened for racing)

Buick side trim

Cadillac sombrero wheel covers

Wide whitewalls

'54 Chevy grille with extra teeth

MONSTER TOUCH CUSTOMIZE

Truck with raised suspension

Truck with lowered suspension

CUSTOMIZING IS ALMOST AS OLD AS THE AUTOMOBILE ITSELF. THERE'S AN HONORABLE TRADITION IN NOT LEAVING WELL ENOUGH ALONE.

Modifying and hot rodding go back to the earliest days of the automobile. Even before cars were commonplace, owners wanted to make theirs different from others. Everybody from Sears to small manufacturers with headquarters in a garage sold accessories and add-ons for the Model T Ford. Mechanically inclined owners tinkered endlessly to make their Ts look and perform the way they wanted, often spending more than the cost of the car on modifications, just like today. The Model T engine remained a favorite of both track racers and street racers well into the 1930s because so much speed equipment was available.

Making a car look and perform the way you want is easier now than ever before, thanks to the industry that grew from those early days.

One of the easiest custom touches to add to any car is a new set of wheels and tires. Wheels are often the first thing a car owner changes; sometimes the only thing. A popular addition today is the large-diameter wheel—18, 20, even 22 inches in diameter—with a wide, low-profile tire.

This idea comes from racing, where large-diameter wheels are needed to fit over large brakes. Low-profile tires on big wheels keep the overall outside diameter a reasonable size and increase sidewall rigidity for better handling. The spoked style of the wheel itself came from racing too.

Some early lightweight wheels were made from magnesium alloy, so all cast-alloy wheels came to be called magnesium, or mag, wheels. Cast wheels are usually made of aluminum alloy now. High-style, high-price billet wheels are machined from solid chunks, or billets, of aluminum, rather than being cast.

Big tachometer
(Shows engine speed)

Custom wheels, radical lowering, high-quality engine and chassis craftsmanship, and custom interiors are some of the additions hot rodders and customizers love. Many rodders and customizers start with simple changes such as a set of custom wheels, paint or vinyl graphics, and some bolt-on body modifications.

MONSTER TOUCH PAINT

Paint is the surest way to make a standout ride. A great paint job attracts attention, whether it's a brilliant candy color that looks elbow-deep and sticky-sweet, trendy pastel graphics and splashes, or fierce flames over basic black.

The art of custom car painting has taken ideas from many fields. Thin painted lines, or pinstriping, decorated pottery and other objects for centuries. Custom painters in the 1950s accented character lines and contours on car bodies with stripes, but then began creating elaborate decorations on hoods and trunk lids. Outlined gold stripes along panel edges were first used on fire engines and circus wagons.

Scallops from airplanes and racecars of the 1930s showed up on 1950s customs, some designs flowed all over the car. Flames appeared about the same time. Both disappeared for a while, but flames are popular again. Tribal graphics and other wildly wandering designs are like the old scallops.

Custom painters also experimented with the paint itself. They developed candy colors (translucent color coats over a reflective gold, silver, copper, or pearl-white base), metal-flake (a reflective paint base that

Upper left: A 350Z takes on a mammal—or perhaps a fish—aura with black stripes over orange paint. *Upper right*: This Caddy sports a teardrop-style flame design. *Lower left*: Black flames look almost like cutouts in the red truck hood, continuing the theme set by the cutouts in the custom grille. *Lower right*: Bold shockwaves accent a striking two-tone treatment.

actually contains flakes of metal), and pearlescent colors. Some car builders simply painted the bodywork with dark gray primer and left it at that. Many street rods had the black suede-looking finish. It often meant that looks didn't matter to the builder—the whole budget went into speed equipment. Today the suede look is popular again. But now instead of primer, it's usually done with more durable black enamel that's deglossed.

Today's factory finishes have the depth and shimmer once available only from a custom painter, so pinstriping, flames, or graphics are often put on over the factory paint job. Vinyl decals and magnetic stick-ons are an easy way to give a car or truck a custom-painted look without using any paint at all.

AN ART THAT KNOWS NO BOUNDS, CUSTOM PAINTING CAN BE SUBTLE OR SPLASHY. EITHER WAY, IT'S SURE TO GET A RIDE NOTICED.

BIG BLOCK A big, heavy engine, such as the 454-cubic-inch Chevrolet or 429/460-cubic-inch Ford. A small-block engine, such as the 350-cubic-inch Chevrolet or 302- cubic-inch Ford, is smaller and lighter. An engine with large displacement isn't always a big block: Some small-blocks exceed 400 CID.

BIG BLOCK

BILLET A single chunk of metal. In *Monster Nation*, the metal is aluminum and the term refers to wheels and other parts and accessories machined or machine-made, from solid chunks of aluminum rather than being forged or cast. Sometimes it just means an item that has been styled to look like it was machined from a single billet.

BILLET

CAMMER An overhead-cam engine. Placing the cam in the cylinder head instead of the engine block lightens the valvetrain, which can improve performance. A single overhead cam (SOHC) operates both intake and exhaust valves. A double overhead cam (DOHC) has one cam for intake valves and one for exhaust valves.

CAT-BACK A performance exhaust system that replaces the pipes and muffler from the catalytic converter to the outlet. A cat-back system usually has large tubing and a free-flowing muffler.

DEUCE A 1932 Ford, not just any old coupe or roadster (or fiberglass replica). The 1932 coupe and roadster are famous, but there are also deuce sedans, pickups, and other body styles.

DISPLACEMENT The total volume of an engine's cylinders, in cubic inches (ci), cubic centimeters (cc), or liters (l). To convert metric displacement in liters to approximate cubic inches, multiply liters times 61. To convert cubic inches to approximate displacement in liters, divide cubic inches by 61. One liter equals 1,000 cc.

FLATHEAD An engine design with the valves in the engine block rather than the head. Engineers call this design, once the usual for production cars, an L-head or side-valve engine. In *Monster Nation*, flathead usually refers to the L-head Ford V-8

manufactured from 1932 to 1953. It was the most often used early hot rod engine.

HEADER An exhaust manifold made from tubing, designed to provide freer flow of exhaust gases than a factory exhaust manifold. Dragster headers—a separate pipe for each exhaust port—are called zoomies.

HEMI The famous Chrysler Firepower V-8. Introduced in 1951, it had combustion chambers shaped like halves of spheres—hemispheres. Along with Dodge and DeSoto engines of similar design, it came to be known as the Hemi. Other engines before and since have had hemispherical combustion chambers, but none have been as well-known for them as the Chrysler engines.

LEAD Autobody solder, commonly used by early customizers to smooth seams and bodywork, a process called *leading*. Thus, a much-modified custom is often called a *leadsled*, even though fiberglass and plastic fillers are now used more than lead.

LOUVERS Ventilating slots punched into a panel, such as a hood. Often they're more for looks than for letting air in or out.

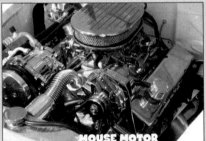

MOUSE MOTOR

MOUSE MOTOR The legendary and widely-used small-block Chevy engine.

NITRO Nitromethane, the fuel for Top Fuel class dragsters and other competition engines. Compared to gasoline, nitro doesn't burn as fast and produces less energy per pound. But because it contains oxygen that helps it burn, 1 pound of nitro needs less than 2 pounds of air for combustion, while 1 pound of gasoline must be mixed with almost 15 pounds of air. A mixture with that much more fuel produces monster power. At about $35 per gallon, nitro is often used only as a fuel additive. But some racing engines run on pure nitro, consuming about a gallon per second. Drivers and crew members wear gas masks because the exhaust gases contain nitric acid vapor.

LOUVERS

NITROUS Nitrous oxide (N_2O), is a gas sprayed into an engine's intake manifold to provide extra oxygen. That oxygen, mixed with additional gasoline sprayed in at the same time, gives a monster power boost—often 100 or more additional horsepower. Nitrous is usually only used for a short burst of power. Also referred to as *juice*, *squeeze*, *the bottle*, *spray*, or *supercharger in a can*.

RAT MOTOR

RAT MOTOR A big-block Chevy engine.

SLAMMED A way-lowered vehicle, one that looks like it's been picked up by a giant and, yes, slammed down onto the ground. The look is also known as *in the weeds*.

SPOILER An aerodynamic device designed to break up airflow over a surface to prevent lift. Wings and other airfoils on cars are not for flying, but to prevent a car from flying off the road. They improve road handling by pushing the vehicle down. Spoilers do the same by reducing lift.

SUPERCHARGER A mechanical device that forces more air-fuel mixture into the engine for increased performance. Often called a blower, it usually sits on top of the engine and is belt-driven. The one often seen on hot rods is actually an exhaust-scavenging pump from a diesel engine.

T-BUCKET A hot rod with a Ford Model T roadster body, no fenders, and lots of engine. The T-bucket style started with a rod built by Norm Grabowski in the 1950s and used in the TV series *77 Sunset Strip*. The T-bucket remains popular and is easy to build because you can buy every part you need new, including the frame and a fiberglass replica body.

TUNER A late-model compact sports coupe or sedan modified for high performance. Tuners are front-wheel drive cars with high-revving small-displacement engines that crank out the kind of performance once reserved for muscle cars. Lowered suspension, high-performance wheels and tires, more powerful brakes, and aerodynamic body modifications are usually part of the overall tuner package. Some cars have the tuner look, but without the engine modifications.

TURBOCHARGER A centrifugal supercharger driven by an exhaust-gas turbine. Turbocharger installations often include an intercooler to cool the intake charge, making it denser and increasing power.